?

TOSSING
THE MASKS

Your Pandemic Recovery Plan

WORKBOOK & JOURNAL

ROBERT MILLER
HENRY PARK

Dedicated to all of the world's dreamers.

The moment you doubt you can fly, you
cease forever to be able to do it.

– J. M. Barrie
Peter Pan

This is my seventh book – my fifth book published during the pandemic – and my fourth book with Henry Park, (I also edited *Henry Park's Road to a Million*). Last July Henry and I published *C19 Economics* – a guide to personal and business finance.

No one ever could have imagined how the pandemic would change our lives. Each of the 8 billion people on Earth has been affected to a different extent and in a different way. Contrary to corporate and government propaganda, we are not "all in this together."

Once the initial shock started to wear off and reality settled in most of us felt like we had fallen down the rabbit hole or had crossed over into *The Twilight Zone.*

Why should this book matter to you? *Tossing the Masks* should matter because it was written with one purpose in mind – to help YOU. The operative word is *help* because we can give you some suggestions but only you can create your post-pandemic life.

Although it may be hard to accept, it's possible that the pandemic may not have changed your life very much. You may have had to *temporarily* change the way you live day-to-day to "survive." But mere survival is not enough – at least it shouldn't be.

Survival boils down everything to the bottom line. For many of us the bottom line over the past eighteen months has been just staying alive – like the Bee Gees song.

Whether you're a brother or whether you're
     a mother
You're stayin' alive, stayin' alive
Feel the city breakin' and everybody
     shakin'
And we're stayin' alive, stayin' alive
Ah, ha, ha, ha, stayin' alive, stayin' alive
Ah, ha, ha, ha, stayin' alive

— *Stayin' Alive* (1977)
Bee Gees

As you read this little book you need to forget about washing your hands, living on take out, hoarding toilet paper, and the pandemic. Whether or not you toss your masks — or do it symbolically — it's time to fuggedaboutit and move on with your life.

Hopefully, the pandemic provided you with the opportunity to reflect on your life, invest in yourself, and make some major changes. If you missed the boat, let's do it!

Here's how to use *Tossing the Masks*. This is a small, simple book written in sixth grade English with large print and a lot of spaces. It's not a textbook – it's a guidebook designed to facilitate (biggest word here) snapping out of the ashes of the pandemic like the Legendary Phoenix and flying to the moon (and beyond). This is an *interactive workbook* which leads you through where you are now to where you want to be. Here are some suggestions. Page through the book once and take note of the parts that interest you. Take ownership of your book – turn down pages, highlight sections, and write in the margins. It's your book – make it an awesome experience.

– Robert Miller

A little over a hundred years ago German writer Franz Kafka published his iconic novella *The Metamorphosis* about a salesman, Gregor Samsa, who woke up one morning as a huge insect and struggled to adjust to his inexplicable transformation which he thought was only temporary.

Like the huge insect Gregor Samsa became, many of us thought that the pandemic would be "temporary" but here we are more than a year later. We "adjusted" our lives to stay safe and keep others safe. Now America is quickly opening back up so it's time for us to get ready. That's what this book is all about — getting ready for what we can and should be the absolute best years of your life.

Our challenge is that there is no "normalcy" and if there was most of us would not want to go back there anyway. Life is – or should be – about moving forward and not about moving backward. **Your Pandemic Recovery Plan** should be all about growth. Take control of your life as quickly as possible, reach for the stars (all of them), revive old dreams (and create new ones), dance on the edge (always), color outside the lines (and erase as many as you can), and get ready to kick some serious ass and take names.

We are going to walk you through **Eleven Magical Steps**: **Wake, Clear, Think, Assess, Consult, Plan, Act, Connect, Change, Live,** and **Prosper**. And we will share some of our magic with you too.

Let's not end up like Kafka's monster who was locked in his room by his family and believed that he had become a burden on his family and eventually starved to death.

Let's take a brief look back in silent prayer to honor those who are no longer with us. Then let's look only forward realizing that we are the future – and the future is us.

Hopefully, like us, you learned a lot of things about yourself (and others) over the course of the pandemic. Let's "accentuate the positives" and "eliminate the negative" like Johnny Mercer's lyrics in the song *Ac-Cent-Tchu-Ate the Positive*. After all, who wants to end life as a starving monstrous insect?

?

TOSSING THE MASKS

Your Pandemic Recovery Plan

WORKBOOK & JOURNAL

ROBERT MILLER
HENRY PARK

Are we tossing the masks or not? It's a 'toss up.' There is no credible or consistent information from the government, the scientific community, or healthcare professionals. In fact, we're suffering from information overload – or **misinformation** overload.

Joe Biden, Dr. Fauci, and the CDC can't seem to get their stories straight. There is a battle between Fox News and CNN and between red and blue. And Facebook has taken it upon themselves to remove 'fake news" from their pages.

The problem is that what might have been 'fake news' yesterday – or even an hour ago – might now be 'real news'. It might be a case of 'no news is good news' because we don't know what to believe.

As this book goes to press America plans to toss the masks. But it's not going to be that simple. There are major political and social divides over masks and vaccinations. And with the lack of leadership on all levels of government the divide is going to continue to become bigger and bigger.

Variants, breakthrough infections, side effects, fear of side effects, and every possible emotion that we might experience will complicate and prolong America's recovery from this pandemic.

And no matter what we do, the prolonged pandemic recovery will have devastating long-term effects on our economy. In the final analysis, the American economy is strong and resilient.

While our economy will *eventually* recover our minds may not. The pandemic has resulted to a dramatic increase in depression, anxiety, and suicidal thoughts. It may be too early to tell but when all the numbers are it they may show that suicides have dramatically increased too.

Physical isolation, social distancing, loss of work, financial challenges, anxiety about catching or spreading the virus, fear of death, and fear of losing loved ones – all are stressing us 24/7. All that is mitigated by confusion about whether to get vaccinated and whether to mask up or not.

What do we do? Each of us must create our own *Pandemic Recovery Plan* to recover financially, resume social activities, and heal from the trauma.

Are we tossing the masks too soon? America and the entire world are so anxious to get back to what we perceive as 'normal' that some of us may be tossing caution to the wind by tossing our masks so soon.

While there may be legitimate concerns about the effectiveness of masks it is a relatively cheap and easy added layer (or layers) of protection.

We have had nothing but mixed messages about the effectiveness (and politics) of masks, risks of masking up and going face-naked, vaccinations and variants. Many people, even healthcare professionals, are not convinced about who vaccines may protect and to what extent. And there are holdouts waiting for *final* FDA approvals beyond the emergency sanctions that were granted. There are anti-vax people but also those who are concerned about both immediate and long-term side effects. And, with many variants rapidly emerging, there are concerns about whether booster shots will be required.

Part of the blame for the curve not staying flattened has to go to the 'vaxholes' who anxiously got jabbed and anxiously tossed their masks as a gesture of liberation.

There is 'mask-shaming' and 'vax-shaming' as the WHO, CDC, and (especially) POTUS continue to vomit propaganda designed to convince, bribe, or threaten everyone to get jabbed ASAP.

Like in sports, the best defense may be a strong well-planned and strategically executed offense. That means blocking out all the static, ignoring the talking heads, and doing your own research by consulting with those you trust within and outside the healthcare world.

We authored this little book to inspire and empower you to slow down, take a deep breath, and evaluate what is the best way to protect yourself and your family. And, to help you organize your thoughts into a plan to recover emotionally and financially from the devastation of the pandemic which shows no signs of ending anytime soon. So, mask up, make a decision about being jabbed, and invest the time and energy to create a plan now.

Behind every mask is a face,
and behind that a story.

– Marty Rubin

There is a fifth dimension, beyond which is known to man. It is a dimension as vast as space and as timeless as infinity. It is the middle ground between light and shadow, between science and superstition, and it lies between the pit of man's fears and the summit of his knowledge.

– Rod Serling
The Twilight Zone

BACK PAGES

You are braver than you believe, stronger than you seem, smarter than you think, and loved more than you'll ever know.

— A. A. Milne

We didn't see it coming. Depending on how you count we either began the last year of the decade — or the beginning of a new one in 2020. It really doesn't matter because, for many of us, it was the beginning of a nightmare that may be far from over. Before we move too far forward it's important to take a brief look at our back pages and think about what we did wrong – and, especially, what we did right. During the pandemic we were told that we can't always get what we wanted – and sometimes what we needed. Relative to what some of us have been through – or what our parents, grandparents, great grandparents – and on and on – have been through the pandemic may not have the worst experience of our lifetimes.

Like most experiences, you get out of it what you put into it. So if you greeted the pandemic with stress and fear that's what you got. But anyway, those are our back pages. Let's focus on the remaining pages of our lives.

Think of this little book as a magical tool that will start you on a journey for the rest of your life. Like falling down the rabbit hole and arriving to Wonderland with Alice. Like being swept away with Dorothy and Toto by a tornado and landing in The Land of Oz. Like flying to Neverland with Peter Pan and the Lost Boys.

Look back on the pandemic nightmare as philosophically as you can. Think back on what you learned. Take a deep breath, pat yourself on the back, hug your loved ones, air high-five your friends, and let's get our lives going again.

We have a fantastic opportunity – and a great responsibility to get ourselves and our country moving again.

Most of us in business and finance believe that things may get worse before they get better. While the curve may be flattening the economy is on the edge.

The biggest two challenges most of us will have pulling out of this nightmare are our emotions and our finances. The last year and a half has been rough.

There is a saying that when you fall off a horse then you get back up as soon as possible – which means NOW. But that's usually said then done. We've been pretty beaten up. Many people are suffering from anxiety and depression.

Many peoples' finances are in the same situation – reserves have been depleted and the outlook for future earnings is uncertain.

As a nation, and individually, we have lost our momentum. And that is not good. The U.S. Economy is like a bullet train that has been forced to slow down.

Momentum is what we need. We need to put the pandemic and all its collateral damage behind us as soon as possible and recover emotionally and financially (as individuals and as a nation).

Contrary to what the Rolling Stones sing *(You Can't Always Get What You Want).* – American's are accustomed to getting what we want.

The opportunities for getting want we want over the next ten years (and well beyond) in America are as unlimited as the universe. $80 Trillion of Baby Boomer Wealth is going to change hands and fortunes will be made in the stock mark and in real estate. Don't believe us? Read *Henry Park's Road to a Million.*

You can't always get what you want
You can't always get what you want
You can't always get what you want
But if you try sometimes, well, you might
    find
You get what you need

    – *You Can't Always Get What You Want* (2016)
                        The Rolling Stones

1

WAKE

Half-wracked prejudice leaped forth, 'rip
down all hate,' I screamed
Lies that life is black and white spoke
from my skull, I dreamed
Romantic facts of musketeers
foundationed deep somehow
Ah, but I was so much older then, I'm
younger than that now

— *My Back Pages* (1964)
Bob Dylan

American Singer-Songwriter Bob Dylan's "dent on the universe" includes 39 studio albums, 95 singles, 52 music videos, 12 live albums, 20 box sets, and seven soundtracks as main contributor. We can learn a lot about ourselves from Dylan's songs and lyrics.

I f you have to look up "Karen" in the Urban Dictionary you may not be as "woke" as you should be. But this is not about "woke" – it's about **WAKE.**

It's time to wake up from the **nightmare** and put together a plan to live your life of your **dreams**. Grab your Bulletproof™ Coffee and a notepad. Find a quiet place and let's get started! And remember to believe!

WAKE

WAKE

2

CLEAR

Relax, allow the mind to become empty, and surprise yourself with the great treasure that begins to flow from your soul.

— Paulo Coelho
The Valkyries (1992)

Paulo Coelho is a Brazilian lyricist and novelist best known for *The Alchemist* (1988) – a captivating and inspirational story about a young boy's journey with the underlying theme that we must pursue our dreams by following what our heart desires. And the bottom line? "To realize one's destiny is a person's obligation."

There may be nothing more beautiful than an empty sky – except perhaps a sky with a full moon. You don't need to completely empty your mind. But you need to clear away all the distractions and focus on what's important in your life. It may be our moon, a planet, stars, or even comets. Don't allow an occasional shooting star – or even a meteor shower – to eclipse your dreams.

CLEAR

CLEAR

3

THINK

And I don't know a soul who's not been
    battered
I don't have a friend who feels at ease
I don't know a dream that's not been
    shattered or driven to its knees
But it's all right, it's all right
We've lived so well so long
Still, when I think of the road we're
      traveling on
I wonder what went wrong
I can't help it, I wonder what went wrong
        — *American Tune* (1972)
        Paul Simon

Paul Simon 's sentiments in *American Tune* are an iconic depiction of how many of us feel right now

O nce you are either "woke" or awake – whichever you prefer – the first thing you have to do is stop and take a big deep breath and **THINK** about the life you want to live. And remember that thinking is not an event – it's a process. Take how much time you need, an hour, a day, a month, a year, to decide exactly what you want and how to get it. Remember that YOU are the Magic!

THINK

THINK

4

ASSESS

Without proper self-evaluation, failure is inevitable.

— John Wooden

Evaluate yourself but don't be too hard on yourself – it is what it is! There's an age-old and very over-used cliché: "Today's the *first* day of the rest of your life. As trite as it might sound it's a powerful reminder that change is a process – not an event. But you have to be able to measure and, more importantly, appreciate your transition from where you are now to where you want to be. Simply stated – who you are now and who you want to be. Tadpole to frog or caterpillar to butterfly? Reach for the stars but keep at least one foot on the ground.

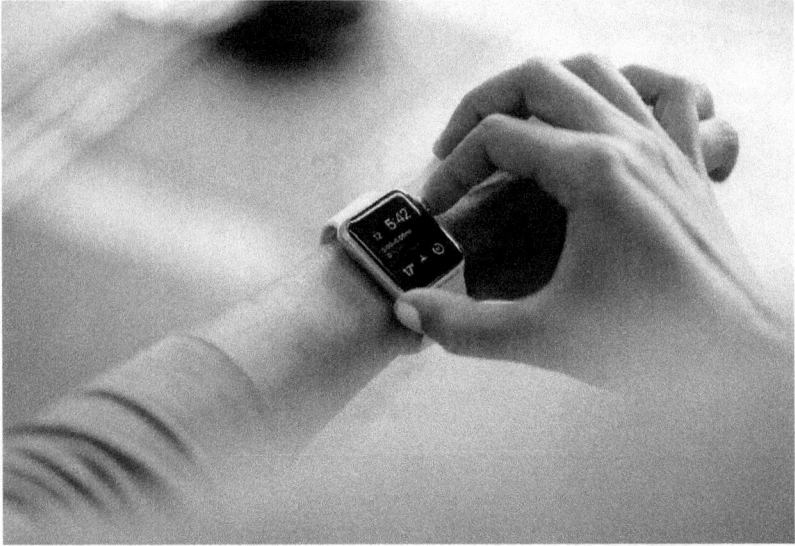

The most important rule of self-assessment is **be true to yourself**. Invest the time and energy to make an honest appraisal of where you are physically, mentally, spiritually, emotionally, and financially.

During the pandemic did you lose money and/or body mass – or did you gain weight and become stressed? Wherever you are now is a fresh start!

ASSESS

ASSESS

5

CONSULT

Beware of lawyers and consultants who do not take risks and do not get their hands dirty.

— Felix Rohatyn

So here's the legal disclaimer that you've been waiting for. These Eleven Magical Steps are far from professional advice. They are – pure and simple – designed to get you thinking and inspire you to create your own personal or business Pandemic Recovery Plan. Once you have completed your self–evaluation and have finished this eBook you should consider seeking some professional advice to help you put together your plan. If you need some help from us please let us know.

CONSULT

S ometimes those of us who need the most help are the most reluctant to seek professional advice. Who are your trusted advisors? Have you met with (or even talked with them) over the course of the pandemic?

Doctor, Lawyer, Indian Chief... As tempting as it might seem Google may not be your best advisor. A team of trusted advisors is vital to your success!

CONSULT

CONSULT

6

PLAN

A goal without a plan is just a wish.
— Antoine de Saint Exupéry

Have you ever read *The Little Prince*? It's a beautiful little book written by French author Antoine de Saint Exupéry in 1943 delivering the moral message that love is priceless and vital to being able to see the beauty of all things. Saint Exupéry was an aviator who looked at danger and adventure through the eyes of a poet and writer. At age 26 he joined the Compagnie Latécoère and helped establish airmail routes over northwest Africa, the South Atlantic, and South America. Can you imagine the flight plans he created? Read his books.

W e are midway through this little book and, as planned, are in the part titled **PLAN**. You can create your personal or business plan in many ways. The most important thing is that you invest the time and energy to create one. Create it as a Word Document and save it on a password-protected flash drive or micro memory card, Take ownership and make it dynamic.

PLAN

PLAN

_____
_____
_____
_____
_____
_____
_____
_____
_____
_____
_____
_____
_____
_____
_____
_____
_____
_____
_____
_____
_____

ACT

7

ACT

The path to success is to take massive, determined action.

— Tony Robbins

All the plans in the world are worthless without massive action. And don't think you have to complete your plan *before* you can take massive action – or any action. Your Personal or Business Pandemic Recovery Plan should be a living dynamic document – always improving like Tony's **CANI** – *constantly and neverending improvement.* Take massive action and keep going. Life, in the final analysis, is all about **ACTION** – or failure to take action. It's always better to do something than do nothing. The more times you fall down the stronger you'll be.

You should always be acting. One of your core values should be **momentum**. Momentum is one of the major keys to success. Many of us have lost our momentum over the course of the pandemic. Have you ever rum a 10K or even a marathon? Some people, when they get tired, walk for a while. Others can never walk because losing momentum is a death wish.

ACT

CONNECT

8

CONNECT

A hug is always the right size.

> — A. A. Milne
> *Winnie the Pooh* (1926)

One of the biggest collateral damages of the pandemic has been reduced human contact. Early in the pandemic Neil Diamond modified the lyrics of *Sweet Caroline* to replace "hands touching hands" with "hands washing hands in a coronavirus version of his iconic song. As much as digital and virtual contact went viral with the virus there was limited hugging. Diamond's lyrics included "don't touch me, I won't touch you." Like the Pooh Bear says – **a hug is always the right size**. And virtual hugs work, too!

This is the time to reconnect. Face-to-face contact is the most effective – and rewarding forms of connecting. After a year and a half or "sheltering in place" and "social distancing" we are all ready to start reconnecting. If you can't meet in person than connect in some other ways. Try a handwritten note or letter or personal email. And phone calls are a great way to reconnect. However, you do it, just connect and reconnect!

CONNECT

CONNECT

9

CHANGE

⇄

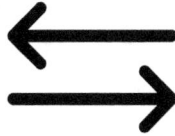

Every success story is a tale of constant adaptation, revision, and change.
— Richard Branson

Change is the best think than can happen to you. You may not be able to change the world – or other people – but you can change yourself and your own life. Life either happens to us or we make life happen. Without change life is boring, stagnant, and often becomes toxic. Changes are what keep us alive. Like **Sir** Richard Branson says, it's all about **adaptation**, **revision**, and **change**. Many of us have succeeded in the development and implementation of those shills during the pandemic.

There are many theories about how long it takes to successfully effect changes that are permanent – AKA habits. Google says: It can take anywhere from 18 to 254 days for a person to form a new habit and an average of 66 daysfor a new behavior to become automatic (Oct. 24, 2019). And that information doesn't really mean anything because we are all different.

CHANGE

CHANGE

10

LIVE

Just living is not enough… one must have sunshine, freedom, and a little flower.
— Hans Christian Anderson

During the pandemic we learned that "just living is not enough…" Although we (hopefully most of us) are grateful for having "survived" the pandemic *survival* should never be the end game. The end game means prosperity. And prosperity doesn't just mean money – prosperity means health, wealth, and happiness. Prosperity is a lifestyle – not a bank account. Prosperity can be what **you** want it to be – freedom, love, passion, travel, abundance, wellness…" You can be as rich as you want to be – it's all up to you.

Is there a better song about **life** than Frank Sinatra's *My Way?* Maybe you prefer the way Elvis sang it – or even Sid Vicious. Any way. *My Way* is a great song, and you should live your life **your way**.

Like most of us you probably have not been able to live your life the way you wanted to live it. Now we're tossing our masks and you can live it your way.

LIVE

LIVE

11

PROSPER

As much as we need a prosperous economy, we also need a prosperity of kindness and decency.

— Caroline Kennedy

You have (or should have by now) your own definition of **prosperity**. In many cultures the pig is a symbol of prosperity, fertility, and good luck. Around the world a piggybank is a symbol of money and putting coins in it shows that we are concerned about our financial futures. There is an old Irish saying: "The pig is the gentleman who pays the rent." Germans say Glücksschwein which means "lucky pig." What does the pig mean to you? And there's nothing wrong with a Capitalist Pig.

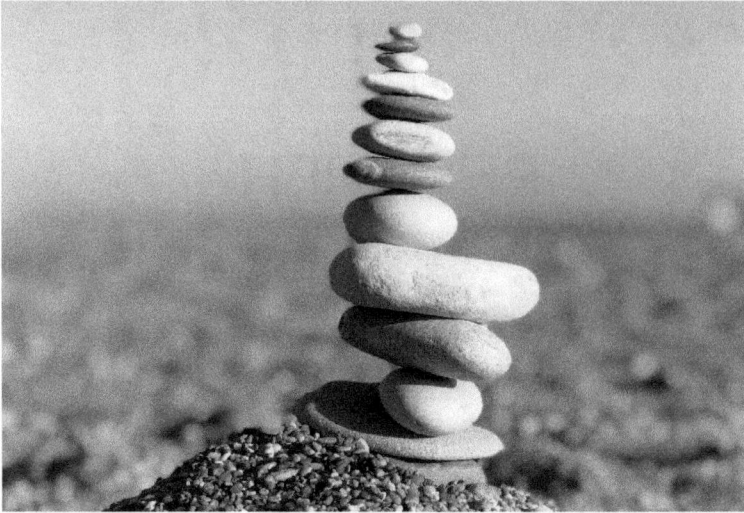

S tacking stones on the beach is an ancient ritual for good fortune and prosperity. Creating your pandemic recovery plan is like stacking stones on the beach.

Picture yourself stacking these eleven stones on the beach: **Wake**, **Clear**, **Think**, **Assess**, **Consult**, **Plan**, **Act**, **Connect**, **Change**, **Live**, and **Prosper**. Take your time – enjoy the experience. Because it's ALL about the *experience.*

PROSPER

PROSPER

What is better – rich or richer? Unless you're already a multi-gazillionaire you should order a copy of *Henry Park's Road to a Million: Workbook and Journal* (available on Amazon.com). This book is not a textbook – it's workbook that was written to accompany Henry Park's Road to a Million Facebook Group and weekly Zoom Investment Classes. There are many roads in life. Dare to be great – take the road less traveled. Along with your **Pandemic Recovery Plan**, *Henry Park's Road to a Million* will guide you to live your life as it can be. What do you think about that?

_____

_____

_____

_____

_____

_____

_____

_____

_____

_____

_____

FINAL THOUGHTS

▶▶▎

No matter how dreary and gray our homes are, we people of flesh and blood would rather live there than in any other country, be it ever so beautiful. There is no place like home.

— Dorothy
The Wizard of Oz (1900)

What have you learned?

_____

_____

_____

_____

_____

_____

_____

CORE VALUES

I shall take the heart. For brains do not make one happy, and happiness is the best thing in the world.

– Tin Man
The Wizard of Oz (1900)

What's important to you?

_____
_____
_____
_____
_____
_____
_____
_____
_____

FINANCIAL PLAN

You've always had the power, my dear, you just had to learn it for yourself.

– Glinda the Good Witch
The Wizard of Oz (1900)

Create a simple financial plan.

_____

_____

_____

_____

_____

_____

_____

_____

_____

_____

IMPACT STATEMENT

♥

A heart is not judged by how much you love; but by how much you are loved by others.

— Frank Morgan

How do you impact the world?

_____

_____

_____

_____

_____

_____

_____

_____

_____

SIDE HUSTLES AND NEW CAREERS

I've missed more than 9,000 shots in my career. I've lost almost 300 games. 26 times, I've been trusted to take the game winning shot and missed. I've failed over and over and over again in my life. And that is why I succeed.

— Michael Jordan

Has your career or financial situation changed during the pandemic? Many people have had to struggle through the year — and many are still struggling. There are a lot of side hustles and many of them have morphed into full time jobs while people are waiting for something "permanent." Here are side hustles that can turn into profitable full-time careers.

JOIN OUR TEAM

Are you interested in a part-time or full-time career in **Mortgages**, **Real Estate**, or **Life Insurance**? Become a **Trusted Advisor**. We will sponsor and train you. **Call us at 949.424.5144**

ROBERT MILLER

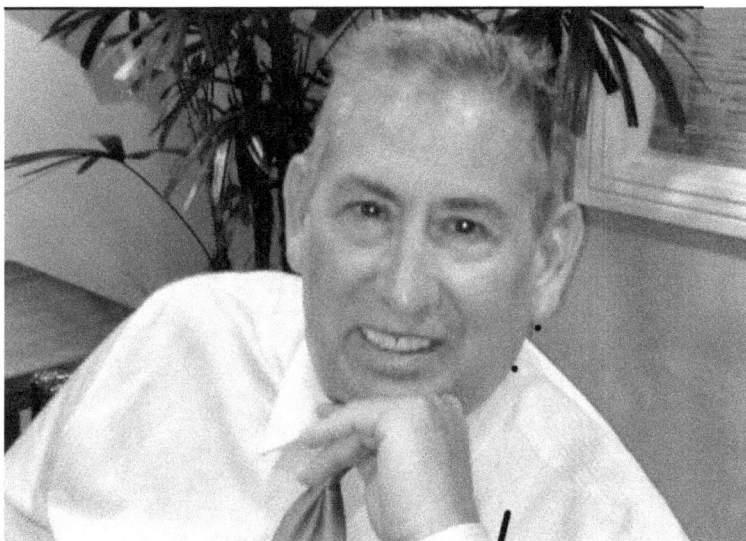

Robert Miller
Financier and Rainmaker
RobertMiller@RobertMiller.com

RobertMiller.com

HENRY PARK

Henry Park
Mortgage Banker, Investor,
and Lifestyle Ambassador

Henry@HenryPark.com

HenryPark.com

MY JOURNAL

Keeping a journal will change your life in ways you'd never imagine.

— Oprah Winfrey

The following 30 pages are for you to keep a journal. If you are already keeping a journal consider keeping a separate one here for the next 30 days – specifically related to your pandemic recovery experience. There is no right way or wrong way to write a journal. Here are some suggestions. Dedicate at least 20 minutes each day to record your thoughts. Find a quiet place. Set your smartphone aside and stay off the grid. You may be a digital person but don't use your phone or computer for this journal. Write or print your journal on these lined pages. Remember it's your journal so you can write whatever you want to write.

61

DATE: _____

DATE: _____

DATE: _____

DATE: _____

DATE: _____

DATE: _____

DATE: _____

DATE: _____

DATE: _____

DATE: _____

DATE: _____

DATE: _____

DATE: _____

DATE: _____

DATE: _____

DATE: _____

DATE: _____

DATE: _____

DATE: _____

DATE: _____

Everyone I know, everywhere I go
People need some reason to believe
I don't know about anyone, but me
If it takes all night, that'll be all right
If I can get you to smile before I leave

— Running on Empty (1977)
Jackson Browne

RESOURCES

A mind is like a parachute, it doesn't work if it isn't open.

— Frank Zappa

The resources available to you on Google, Zoom, YouTube and Amazon are like the Welcome Brunch Buffet at the Royal Hawaiian in Waikiki — there are way too many choices. You can only digest so much. There are Books, Songs, TED Talks, Podcasts, Seminars, Conferences, Videos — and the whole world of the Internet and social media.

Our times are robust with great people whose stories are legendary — from living icons like Oprah to those who live with us in our memories like Steve Jobs. Here are four influencers you should follow.

DANIEL AMEN

The "18/40/60" rule to happiness: At age 18, people care very much about what others think about them. By age 40, they learn not to worry what others think. By age 60, they figure out that no one was thinking about them in the first place.

— Daniel Amen

Daniel Amen is an American celebrity doctor and founder and Director of the Amen Clinics. He is a psychiatrist and brain disorder specialist. Check out his latest bestselling book: *Your Brain is Always Listening* (2021)

VISHEN LAKHIANI

Epic things start with small humble steps. Pay respect to your beginnings. And if you're just starting out, know that it's okay to be sucky. To be small. To be messy and chaotic. Just make sure you never stop dreaming.

— Vishen Lakhiani

Vishen Lakhiani is the founder and CEO of Mindvalley — a platform focused on self-development (mindvalley.com). Check out his latest book — *The Buddha and the Badass: The Secret Spiritual Art of Succeeding at Work* (2020).

SIMON SINEK

?

People don't buy what you do; they buy why you do it. And what you do simply proves what you believe.

— Simon Sinek

Simon Sinek is the author of five books, including *Start With Why* (2009) – his first book. His TEDx conferences are on YouTube. Check out simonsinek.com.

o

TONY ROBBINS

S uccess is doing what you want to do, when you want, with whom you want.

— Tony Robbins

Tony Robbins is simply Tony Robbins.

There is no other way to describe him.

Tony Robbins is an amazing influencer.

Watch the Netflix Documentary *I Am Not Your Guru* and check out tonyrobbins.com and "Ignite. Achieve. Excel."

MY RESOURCES

MY RESOURCES

Well those drifter's days are past me now
I've got so much more to think about
Deadlines and commitments
What to leave in and what to leave out

Against the wind
I'm still runnin' against the wind
I'm older now and still running against the
    wind

– *Against the Wind* (1980)
Bob Seger & The Silver Bullet Band

www.ingramcontent.com/pod-product-compliance
Lightning Source LLC
LaVergne TN
LVHW051655080426
835511LV00017B/2582